Houghton
Mifflin
Harcourt

NATIONAL JOURNEYS

Program Consultants
Shervaughnna Anderson · Marty Hougen
Carol Jago · Erik Palmer · Shane Templeton
Sheila Valencia · MaryEllen Vogt
Consulting Author · Irene Fountas

Unit 6

Three Cheers for Us!

Owl at Home

CHAPTER BOOK

by Arnold Lobel

Be a Reading Detective!

Welcome, Reader!

Your help is needed to find clues in texts. As a **Reading Detective**, you will need to **ask lots of questions**. You will also need to **read carefully**.

myNotebook

As you read, mark up the text. Save your work to **myNotebook**.

- Highlight details.
- Add notes and questions.
- Add new words to **myWordList**.

- Use letters and sounds you know to help you read the words.

- Look at the pictures.

- Think about what is happening.

Let's go!

UNIT 6

Three Cheers for Us!

Stream to Start

Performance Task Preview

At the end of this unit, you will write an opinion paragraph about learning to do something new! In your paragraph, you will use details from the texts you read.

hmhfyi.com

Channel One News®

9

Talk About Words
Work with a partner. Choose one of the **Context Cards.** Add words to the sentence to tell more about the photo.

📓 myNotebook

Add new words to **myWordList**. Use them in your speaking and writing.

Words to Know

▶ **Read each Context Card.**

▶ **Choose two blue words. Use them in sentences.**

1 **teacher**
The art teacher shows how to use a brush.

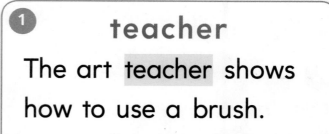

2 **studied**
She studied the flower before she drew it.

3 **surprised**

He was surprised to see such a big statue.

4 **toward**

He walked slowly toward the art table.

5 **bear**

The picture of the bear looks very real.

6 **above**

These shapes hang high above the floor.

7 **even**

This box has even more crayons in it.

8 **pushed**

He pushed the clay into new shapes.

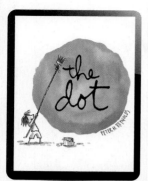

Read and Comprehend

☑ **TARGET SKILL**

Compare and Contrast As you read, ask yourself how things are alike and different. Good readers use text evidence to **compare** and **contrast** characters, settings, or events. To understand a story better, use a diagram to show how two things are alike and different.

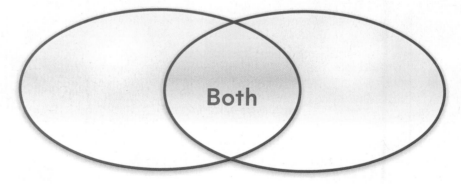

Both

☑ **TARGET STRATEGY**

Monitor/Clarify If a part doesn't make sense, reread it, ask and answer questions about it, and use the pictures for help.

Visual Arts

There are many ways to make art. You can use crayons or markers to draw. You can paint a picture. You could cut shapes out of paper and glue them together. A computer can be used to draw and find pictures for artwork. You will find out how one girl makes art in **The Dot.**

Think | Draw | Pair | Share

What are some ways you like to make art? Think about it. Draw a picture. Tell a partner about your picture. Show your picture as you talk to explain.

ANCHOR TEXT

✓ **GENRE**

Realistic fiction is a story that could happen in real life. As you read, look for:

▶ characters who act as real people do

▶ events that could really happen

Meet the Author and Illustrator

Peter H. Reynolds

It took Peter H. Reynolds a year and a half to write **The Dot**. He named his character Vashti after a young girl he met at a coffee shop. Mr. Reynolds wrote **Ish** as a follow-up book to **The Dot**.

the dot

by Peter H. Reynolds

ESSENTIAL QUESTION

What are some different ways to make art?

Art class was over, but Vashti sat glued to her chair.

Her paper was empty.

ANALYZE THE TEXT

Figurative Language
What does being "glued to your chair" mean?

Vashti's teacher leaned over the blank paper.
"Ah! A polar bear in a snow storm," she said.
"Very funny!" said Vashti. "I just CAN'T draw!"

Her teacher smiled.

"Just make a mark and
see where it takes you."

Vashti grabbed a marker and
gave the paper a good, strong jab.

"There!"

Her teacher picked up the paper
and studied it carefully.

"Hmmmmm."

She pushed the paper toward
Vashti and quietly said,
"Now sign it."

Vashti thought for a moment.

"Well, maybe I can't draw,
but I CAN sign my name."

The next week,
when Vashti walked into art class,
she was surprised to see what was
hanging above her teacher's desk.

It was the little dot
she had drawn—HER DOT!
All framed in swirly gold!

"Hmmph!
I can make a better dot than THAT!"

She opened her
never-before-used set of
watercolors and set to work.

Vashti painted and painted.
A red dot. A purple dot.
A yellow dot. A blue dot.

The blue mixed with the yellow.
She discovered that she could make
a GREEN dot.

Vashti kept experimenting.
Lots of little dots in many colors.

"If I can make little dots,
I can make BIG dots, too."

Vashti splashed her colors with
a bigger brush on bigger paper
to make bigger dots.

Vashti even made a dot
by NOT painting a dot.

At the school art show a few weeks later,
Vashti's many dots made quite a splash.

Vashti noticed a little boy gazing up at her.

"You're a really great artist.
I wish I could draw," he said.

"I bet you can," said Vashti.

"ME? No, not me. I can't draw
a straight line with a ruler."

Vashti smiled.

She handed the boy
a blank sheet of paper.
"Show me."

The boy's pencil shook
as he drew his line.

Vashti stared at the boy's squiggle.
And then she said . . .

"Sign it."

Dig Deeper

Read Together

Use Clues to Analyze the Text

Use these pages to learn about Compare and Contrast and Figurative Language. Then read **The Dot** again.

Compare and Contrast

When you **compare** and **contrast**, you tell how things are alike and different.

Think about what Vashti is like at the beginning of **The Dot**. She changes by the end of the story. Use a diagram to tell what she is like at the beginning and at the end. Also, tell what things about her stay the same during both parts of the story.

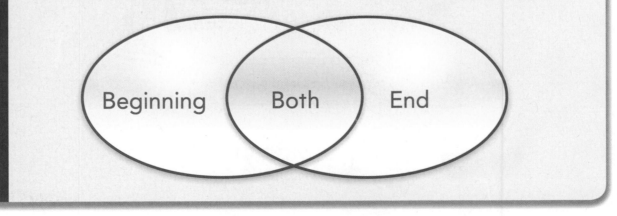

Beginning   Both   End

Figurative Language

Authors sometimes use words that have more than one meaning. In **The Dot**, the author writes that Vashti's dot pictures **made quite a splash** at the art show. The author does not mean that her pictures made people wet. He means that Vashti's pictures are amazing and surprising, like a big splash! What other words mean something else in this story?

Your Turn

RETURN TO THE ESSENTIAL QUESTION

Turn and Talk

What are some different ways to make art? Think about how Vashti makes her art. How do you think the little boy at the end of the story will make art? What other ways could they create art?

💬💬 Classroom Conversation

Talk about these questions with your class.

1 How does Vashti's art teacher help her?

2 How are Vashti's paintings alike? How are they different?

3 How are Vashti and the little boy alike?

WRITE ABOUT READING

Response Choose one piece of Vashti's art. What colors and shapes do you see? How did she make it? Discuss your ideas with a partner. Then write sentences to describe the artwork. Use text evidence to explain your ideas.

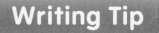

Writing Tip

Add details like adjectives to tell more information about the artwork.

BIOGRAPHY

Read
Together

Artists
Create Art!

☑ GENRE

A **biography** tells about events in a real person's life. This selection tells about more than one artist. Find facts about the artists' lives.

☑ TEXT FOCUS

Captions tell more information about a photo or picture. Use the captions and photos to find out more about the pieces of art.

Artists Create Art!

by Anne Rogers

An artist makes art. Some artists paint pictures. Other artists make things.

David Wynne made this grizzly bear. It stands above a pond in New York.

David Wynne's sculpture "Grizzly Bear" is at the Donald M. Kendall Sculpture Gardens.

Seated Figures, Study for "A Sunday Afternoon on the Island of the Grande Jatte" **by Georges Seurat**

Georges Seurat went to art school in France. Look at his painting. Once you have studied it, you will see it is made of many brushstrokes. Are you surprised?

Tressa "Grandma" Prisbrey used glass bottles to make her art. She learned by herself. No teacher helped her.

Grandma Prisbrey made the wishing well shown below. She even made a building where her grandchildren played.

wishing well

What kind of art would you like to make? Would you like to paint? Would you like to build something? There are many kinds of art!

Compare Texts

Read Together

TEXT TO TEXT

Compare Artworks How are the artworks in the two selections alike? Which artist from **Artists Create Art!** do you think Vashti would like? Tell why.

TEXT TO SELF

Talk About Feelings How do you feel when you try your best? Take turns sharing ideas with a partner.

TEXT TO WORLD

Talk About Art Where have you seen artwork? Have you seen it at school, at home, or in your town? Tell about what you saw.

Grammar

Exclamations A sentence that shows a strong feeling is called an **exclamation.** An exclamation begins with a capital letter and ends with an exclamation point.

Read Together

You are a great artist**!**

That is such a beautiful painting**!**

Art class is so much fun**!**

Try This!

Write each exclamation correctly.
Use another sheet of paper.

1. i can't wait for our school art show

2. this will be the best show ever

3. we are going to have a great time

4. that drawing Ramon made is so tiny

5. it is my very favorite in the show

Connect Grammar to Writing

When you revise your writing, try using exclamations to make it exciting. End each one with an exclamation point.

Opinion Writing

☑ Conventions When you write **opinion sentences,** you can help readers hear your writing voice. Use exclamations to show your strong feelings.

Jill wrote an opinion about Vashti. Then she changed a sentence to an exclamation.

Revised Draft

really great !

I think Vashti is a ~~good~~ artist.

Writing Checklist

 Conventions Did I use exclamations to show my strong feelings?

 Are there any sentences that do not help explain my opinion? Did I delete them?

 Did I use the correct end marks?

In Jill's final copy, how does she show that she feels strongly about her opinion? Now edit your writing. Use the Checklist.

Final Copy

A Great Artist

I think Vashti is a really great artist!

One reason is that she thinks of lots of ways to paint dots.

Another reason is that her paintings are very colorful.

I would like to paint like Vashti.

WHAT CAN YOU DO?
A BOOK ABOUT DISCOVERING WHAT YOU DO WELL

The
Wind and the Sun
an Aesop's fable

🔍 LANGUAGE DETECTIVE

Talk About Words
Work with a partner.
Choose your favorite
photo. Tell why it's
your favorite. Use as
many of the blue words
as possible. Be sure to
use complete sentences.

Words to Know

Read Together

▶ Read each **Context Card**.

▶ Make up a new sentence
that uses a blue word.

1 **different**

These friends help sort
things in different bins.

2 **near**

The girl helps plant
flowers near the porch.

3 enough

Is there **enough** paint for everyone?

4 stories

They read silly **stories** to each other.

5 high

The girl helped him swing **high**!

6 always

She **always** helps her brother tie his shoes.

7 once

The boys cleaned up **once** they were done.

8 happy

She was **happy** to help wash the dog.

Read and Comprehend

Read Together

☑ **TARGET SKILL**

Author's Purpose Authors may write to make you laugh or to give information. An author's reason for writing is called the **author's purpose.** As you read, use important details to help you figure out what the authors want you to learn. List the details in a chart.

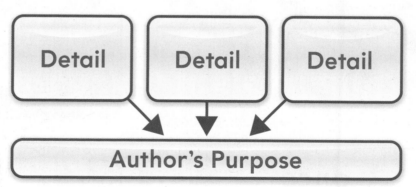

☑ **TARGET STRATEGY**

Analyze/Evaluate Tell what you think and feel about the selection. Give text evidence to tell why.

Trying Hard

Learning something new can be hard work. Learning to ride a bike takes practice. Learning to snap your fingers does, too. Not many people can do it the first time they try.

In **What Can You Do?**, you will find out what different children can do. Find out how they learn new things.

💬 Talk About It

What can you do now because you kept trying? Write your answer. Then share your ideas with your classmates.

ANCHOR TEXT

WHAT
CAN YOU DO?
A BOOK ABOUT DISCOVERING WHAT YOU DO WELL
BY SHELLEY ROTNER AND SHEILA KELLY · PHOTOGRAPHS BY SHELLEY ROTNER

☑ GENRE

Informational text gives facts about a topic. Look for:
- information and facts in the words
- photographs that show the real world

Meet the Author and Photographer
Shelley Rotner

Shelley Rotner is both an author and an award-winning photographer. She has taken photographs of children from around the world.

Meet the Author
Sheila M. Kelly

What a team! Together, Sheila M. Kelly and Shelley Rotner have written about moms, dads, and grandparents. In this book, the two authors show that everyone has talents.

WHAT CAN YOU DO?

A BOOK ABOUT DISCOVERING WHAT YOU DO WELL

BY SHELLEY ROTNER AND SHEILA KELLY, ED.D.

PHOTOGRAPHS BY SHELLEY ROTNER

ESSENTIAL QUESTION

Why is it important to try your best?

"I know a boy
who can draw very
well and a girl who can
climb very high."

"We are all good at doing something.
We're always learning new things
as we get older."

ANALYZE THE TEXT

Author's Purpose Why do you think
the authors wrote this selection?
What details help you know?

"I like to swim
and learned how to float.
I had to practice.
Once I learned, I
felt like I could float for hours!"

"My little brother
is better on skis.
He can ski much faster
than I can."

We're happy when we
do something well,
whatever that might be.

"Reading is easy for me,
but math is much harder.
I'd like to be better at math, though."

"I can't read very well yet.
I wish I could."

It can take a long time
to be good at something.
If we practice, things get
easier and easier to do.

Marie knows how to spell, and Jill prints well. Gene is really good at anything that has to do with computers.

"I haven't
discovered what
I'm good at yet."

Nathan writes funny stories about science.
Some of the funniest ones are
about a baby robot!
Beth likes to build.
The biggest tower she ever built
was taller than she is!

"I made the soccer team this year.
I hope I play well enough to score a goal."
"I see lots of things in the park.
I look near and far.
Things look much closer
through my binoculars!"

We all like to do what we do best.
When things are hard,
we need help to learn.
We might say, "I don't get it."

We're good at different things.

"I feed the baby myself now. When she gets bigger, she will not need help."

"I can fix my brother's wagon. I'm younger than my brother, but I'm good at fixing things."

"I got my training wheels off earlier than I thought I would.
I felt very proud!"

"The kids made me captain of our team. That was one of the happiest days of my life."

ANALYZE THE TEXT

Using Context What does it mean to be the **captain** of a team? What clues help you know?

We have schoolwork, acting, singing,
dancing, playing games, or sports!
We all have something we do well.

What can you do?

Dig Deeper

Use Clues to Analyze the Text

Use these pages to learn about
Author's Purpose and Using Context.
Then read **What Can You Do?** again.

Author's Purpose

Authors write for different reasons. In
What Can You Do? the authors give
information. Why do you think the authors
wrote the selection? What did they want
you to learn? Look for details and text
evidence in the selection that help explain
the topic. You can use a chart to list
details and the authors' purpose.

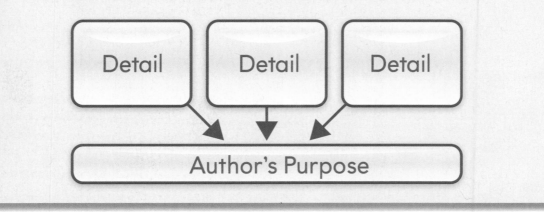

Using Context

When you don't know what a word means, read the sentence again. Ask and answer these questions.

- What clues do I find in the words?
- What clues do I see in the pictures?

In the selection, a girl learns to **float**. You can use the word **swim** and the picture of the girl in water to figure out that **float** means "to rest on the top of the water."

Your Turn

RETURN TO THE ESSENTIAL QUESTION

 **Why is it important to try your best?** Take turns with a partner. Tell what you learned about trying hard from the photos and words in **What Can You Do?** Add your ideas to what your partner says.

💬 Classroom Conversation

Talk about these questions with your class.

1 What can the children in the selection do?

2 How did the children learn how to do new things?

3 Which things from the selection would you like to learn? How will you get started?

WRITE ABOUT READING

Response Write about a time you learned to do something new. Tell what you learned and how you learned it. How did you feel when you knew that you could do it? Draw a picture to go with your sentences.

Writing Tip

Use words to tell about feelings to make your sentences clearer.

FABLE

The
Wind and the Sun
an Aesop's fable

Read Together

☑ GENRE

A **fable** is a short story in which a character learns a lesson.

☑ TEXT FOCUS

In a fable, a character learns a **story lesson**. This lesson is sometimes called a moral. What lesson can you learn from this fable?

Readers' Theater

The Wind and the Sun

an Aesop's fable

Cast

📖 **Narrator**

🌀 **Wind**

☀️ **Sun**

👒 **Traveler**

📖 **Narrator** Sometimes stories teach a lesson. In this story, Wind and Sun have different ideas about who is stronger.

🌀 **Wind** I am stronger.

Sun No, I am stronger.

Wind That's enough bragging. Let's have a contest. I know **I** will win.

Sun I'll be happy to have a contest.

Wind Okay. I see a traveler coming near. Whoever gets the traveler to take off that coat is stronger.

Narrator First Wind began to blow very hard. Once Wind started, it did not stop.

Traveler That wind is always so cold. I need to wrap my coat tight around me.

Narrator Then Sun began to shine from high up in the sky. It was shining gently. The air got warmer and warmer.

Traveler Now it's nice and warm. I can take off my heavy coat.

Narrator The moral is: "It is better to use kindness instead of force."

Compare Texts

Read
Together

TEXT TO TEXT

Compare Characters Talk with a group.
How are the Wind and the Sun like
the children in **What Can You Do?**

TEXT TO SELF

Write About Yourself Write sentences
that tell what you do best. Use
adjectives to describe what you do.
Draw a picture to show what you mean.

TEXT TO WORLD

Connect to Social Studies Think of
a person you know who tries hard.
Write to explain how that person does
his or her best.

Grammar

Kinds of Sentences Different kinds of sentences have different jobs. Every sentence begins with a capital letter and ends with an end mark.

Read Together

A **statement** tells something. She is in a play.
A **question** asks something. Would you like to be in a play?
An **exclamation** shows a strong feeling. I love acting in plays!
A **command** tells someone to do something. Be quiet during the play.

Read each sentence aloud to yourself.
Write it correctly on a sheet of paper.

1. Emma can climb so high

2. did Jamal learn to ski

3. my friend builds things?

4. do your best work

Write these compound sentences.
Add words to tell more.

5. Put _____ paint on your brush, and paint a picture of _____.

6. I ran _____, and I jumped so _____!

Connect Grammar to Writing

When you revise your writing, use different kinds of sentences to make it interesting.

Opinion Writing

☑ Conventions Good **opinion sentences** give reasons. Sometimes you can explain a reason by using the word **because.**

Raul wrote an opinion about skiing. Then he added words to explain his first reason.

Revised Draft

because you can go fast
It is exciting.
⌄

Writing Checklist

Conventions Did I use the word **because** to explain one reason?

 Does my topic sentence tell my opinion?

☑ Did I retell my main idea at the end?

☑ Did I check my spelling with a dictionary?

What words does Raul use to explain why skiing is exciting? Now revise your sentences. Use the Checklist.

Final Copy

Fun on Skis

Skiing is so much fun!

It is exciting because you can go fast.

I also like jumping over big piles of snow.

I am glad that I learned how to ski.

Days With Frog and Toad
by Arnold Lobel

Measuring Weather

🔍 LANGUAGE DETECTIVE

Talk About Words
Work with a partner.
Use two of the blue
words in the same
complete sentence.

Words to Know

▶ Read each **Context Card**.

▶ Ask a question that uses one of the blue words.

1 **second**
The boy is trying to tie his **second** sneaker.

2 **ball**
She practiced until she could hit the **ball** well.

3 across

The runners dashed across the finish line.

4 head

He hit the ball with his head to make a goal.

5 heard

The children heard clapping at the end.

6 large

It was not too hard to ride up the large hill.

7 cried

"We can do it!" cried the team.

8 should

The teacher said that she should try again.

Read and Comprehend

✓ **TARGET SKILL**

Story Structure A story has different parts. **Characters** are the people and animals in a story. The **setting** is when and where a story takes place. The **plot** tells about the problem the characters have and how they solve it. Use a story map to tell about the characters, setting, and plot.

Characters	Setting
Plot	
Problem:	
How it is solved:	

✓ **TARGET STRATEGY**

Infer/Predict Use text evidence to figure out more about the story and to think of what might happen next.

Weather

Weather can cause problems. Storms can damage homes. Too much rain can lead to floods. The weather can also help us. Rain helps crops grow. Wind helps us fly kites. You will find out if the wind helps Frog and Toad in **The Kite.**

💬 Think | Pair | Share

What are some other ways that weather helps us? Think about it. Complete the sentences. Share with a partner.

Weather helps us ___.
Weather doesn't help us ___. ___ is better than ___.

ANCHOR TEXT

Days With Frog and Toad

by Arnold Lobel

✅ GENRE

A **fantasy** story could not happen in real life. As you read, look for:
- events that could not really happen
- animals who talk and act like people

Meet the Author and Illustrator

Arnold Lobel

Arnold Lobel drew many animals before he came up with the Frog and Toad characters. During vacations with his family in Vermont, Mr. Lobel watched his children play with frogs and toads. Soon the animals were starring in his books.

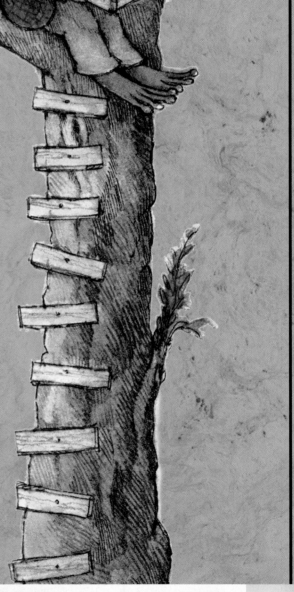

The Kite
from
Days with
Frog and Toad

by Arnold Lobel

ESSENTIAL QUESTION

How can weather
change your day?

The Kite

Frog and Toad went out
to fly a kite.
They went to a large meadow
where the wind was strong.
"Our kite will fly up and up,"
said Frog.
"It will fly all the way up
to the top of the sky."
"Toad," said Frog,
"I will hold the ball of string.
You hold the kite and run."

Toad ran across the meadow.
He ran as fast as his short legs
could carry him.
The kite went up in the air.
It fell to the ground with a bump.
Toad heard laughter.
Three robins were sitting in a bush.

"That kite will not fly,"
said the robins.
"You may as well give up."

Toad ran back to Frog.
"Frog," said Toad,
"this kite will not fly. I give up."

ANALYZE THE TEXT

Story Structure What problem
do Frog and Toad have?

"We must make a second try," said
Frog. "Wave the kite over your head.
Perhaps that will make it fly."

Toad ran back across the meadow.
He waved the kite over his head.

The kite went up in the air
and then fell down with a thud.
"What a joke!" said the robins.
"That kite will never
get off the ground."

Toad ran back to Frog.
"This kite is a joke," he said.
"It will never get off the ground."
"We have to make
a third try," said Frog.
"Wave the kite over your head
and jump up and down.
Perhaps that will make it fly."

Toad ran across the meadow again.
He waved the kite over his head.
He jumped up and down.
The kite went up in the air and
crashed down into the grass.

"That kite is junk," said the robins.
"Throw it away and go home."
Toad ran back to Frog.
"This kite is junk," he said.
"I think we should throw
it away and go home."

"Toad," said Frog,
"we need one more try.
Wave the kite over your head.
Jump up and down
and shout UP KITE UP."

Toad ran across the meadow.
He waved the kite over his head.
He jumped up and down.
He shouted, "UP KITE UP!"

The kite flew into the air.
It climbed higher and higher.
"We did it!" cried Toad.

"Yes," said Frog.
"If a running try
did not work,
a running and waving try
did not work,
and a running, waving,
and jumping try
did not work,
I knew that
a running, waving, jumping,
and shouting try
just had to work."

ANALYZE THE TEXT

Genre: Fantasy How is this story different from **What Can You Do?**

The robins flew out of the bush.
But they could not fly
as high as the kite.
Frog and Toad sat
and watched their kite.
It seemed to be flying
way up at the top of the sky.

Dig Deeper

Use Clues to Analyze the Text

Use these pages to learn about Story Structure and Fantasy. Then read **The Kite** again.

Story Structure

Characters are the people and animals in a story. The **setting** is when and where a story takes place. Where do Frog and Toad try to fly their kite? Is it day or night? The **plot** is the important events. Think about Frog and Toad's problem. How do they solve it? Use a story map to list the parts of the story.

Characters	Setting
Plot	
Problem: How it is solved:	

Genre: Fantasy

Think about the people in **What Can You Do?** from Lesson 27. How are they different from the characters in **The Kite?**

The Kite is a **fantasy.** The story events could not happen in real life. In this story, Frog and Toad talk to each other and do things that people would do. How would a real frog or toad act?

Your Turn

RETURN TO THE ESSENTIAL QUESTION

Turn and Talk

How can weather change your day? How does the weather change Frog and Toad's day? How is the setting important to what happens? Describe the setting using text evidence such as words and pictures.

💬 Classroom Conversation

Talk about these questions with your class.

1 How do the robins act toward Frog and Toad?

2 What do Frog and Toad do to try to get the kite to fly?

3 What really makes the kite fly?

WRITE ABOUT READING ···

Response Write sentences to describe how Frog and Toad are alike and how they are different. Use words and pictures from the story for ideas.

Writing Tip

You can use **like** and **and** to tell how things are alike. Use **not** and **but** to tell how things are different.

Read Together

Measuring Weather

✅ GENRE

Informational text gives facts about a topic. Find facts about weather in this article.

✅ TEXT FOCUS

A **graph** is a drawing that uses numbers, colors, pictures, or symbols to give information. What does the graph on p. 108 show?

Measuring Weather

There are different tools for measuring weather.

Have you ever heard of a windsock? It shows which way the wind blows.

A rain gauge measures how much rain falls. A large storm will bring a lot of rain.

A thermometer measures temperature. Temperature is how warm or cool something is.

On a hot day, you and your friends might like to ride bikes or play ball.

On a cold day, you might want to put on a coat and play in the leaves or build a snowman.

When you know the temperature, you know what to wear.

Look at the bars across the graph.
Each bar shows the temperature for a day.
Which day was the hottest? Which day
was the coolest? What was the temperature
on the second day of the week?

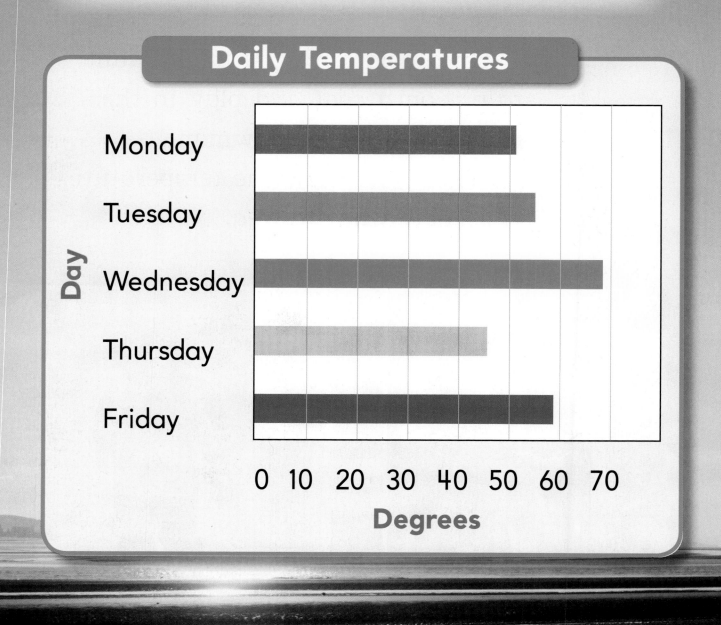

Daily Temperatures

Day

Monday

Tuesday

Wednesday

Thursday

Friday

0 10 20 30 40 50 60 70

Degrees

Compare Texts

Read Together

TEXT TO TEXT

Write to Describe Think about what you learned in **Measuring Weather.** What was the weather like when Frog and Toad flew a kite? Write about it.

TEXT TO SELF

Tell Where You Live Draw a picture that shows the different kinds of weather in your state. Tell about it.

TEXT TO WORLD

Compare Stories Frog and Toad like the outdoors. How is **The Garden** from Lesson 21 like **The Kite**? How is it different? How do the characters act?

Grammar

Kinds of Adjectives Some adjectives describe by telling how things **taste, smell, sound,** or **feel**.

Read Together

Taste	We ate **sweet** berries before we flew kites.
Smell	The air smelled **fresh** and **clean**.
Sound	We gave a **loud** cheer when our kites flew up!
Feel	The **warm** sun shined down on us.

Work with a partner. Find the adjective in each sentence. Decide if it tells how something tastes, smells, sounds, or feels. Then use the adjective in a new sentence.

1. Sam shared his sour pickles at our picnic.

2. Our kites flew in the cool breeze.

3. Some crickets made noisy chirps.

4. We ate some salty chips.

5. Our pie smelled delicious!

Connect Grammar to Writing

When you revise your writing, look for places to add adjectives to tell how things taste, smell, sound, or feel.

Opinion Writing

 Elaboration When you write **opinion sentences,** don't keep using the same words. Use different words to tell more.

Matt wrote about the robins. Later, he changed words to make his ideas clearer.

Revised Draft

The three robins were mean.
laughed at Frog and Toad.
They ~~did mean things.~~
        ∧

Writing Checklist

 Elaboration Did I add adjectives and other exact words to make my ideas clear?

☑ Did I write reasons that explain my opinion?

☑ Does my last sentence retell the main idea?

☑ Did I spell my words correctly?

Which words in Matt's final copy explain how the robins were mean? Now revise your own writing. Use the Checklist.

Final Copy

The Mean Robins

The three robins in the story
<u>The Kite</u> were mean.
They laughed at Frog and Toad.
The noisy, rude robins said that
Frog and Toad's kite was junk.
I would not like to be friends
with those mean robins.

HI! FLY GUY

Tedd Arnold

Busy Bugs

🔍 **LANGUAGE DETECTIVE**

Talk About Words
Verbs are words that
tell what people and
animals do. Work with
a partner. Find the
blue words that are
verbs. Use them in
complete sentences.

Words to Know

Read Together

▶ **Read each Context Card.**

▶ **Describe a picture, using the blue word.**

---

1 **caught**

The spider caught a
bug in its web.

---

2 **took**

I took ladybugs to
show and tell.

3 listen

Listen to the bees buzzing.

4 thought

She thought the spider was scary.

5 minute

I watched the spider in the web for a minute.

6 beautiful

The butterfly is beautiful.

7 idea

Here is an idea, or plan, for a project.

8 friendship

Our friendship is strong.

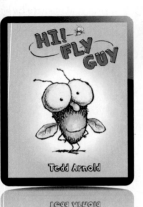

Read and Comprehend

Read Together

☑ TARGET SKILL

Understanding Characters Remember that you can learn a lot about what story characters are like from what they say and do. Good readers use text evidence to figure out how characters feel and why they act the way they do. List clues about the characters in a chart.

Words	Actions	Feelings

☑ TARGET STRATEGY

Visualize To understand a story, picture in your mind what is happening as you read.

Insects

Insects are amazing! An ant can lift as much as ten times its weight. Ladybugs have pretty black spots on their red backs. Bees make honey.

You will read about a boy and an insect he finds in **Hi! Fly Guy.**

💬 Talk About It

What do you know about insects? Complete the sentences: I know insects ___. I would like to know more about ___.

Talk about your ideas.

- ▸ Take turns speaking.
- ▸ Listen carefully.
- ▸ Ask questions.
- ▸ Answer questions.

ANCHOR TEXT

HI! FLY GUY

Tedd Arnold

✅ GENRE

In a **chapter book,** the story is broken up into parts. Look for:
- ► the word **Chapter** and a number
- ► new events in the next chapter

Meet the Author and Illustrator

Tedd Arnold

Tedd Arnold studied art at the University of Florida. He has written and illustrated more than fifty books. Many of them are about Fly Guy. Mr. Arnold lives with his wife Carol, two sons, three cats, and one dog in Elmira, New York.

HI! FLY GUY

by Tedd Arnold

ESSENTIAL QUESTION

How can insects
be helpful?

Chapter 1

A fly went flying.

He was looking for something to eat—

something tasty,

something slimy.

ANALYZE THE TEXT

Author's Word Choice Which word has to do with taste? Which word has to do with touch?

A boy went walking.

He was looking for something

to catch—

something smart,

something for

The Amazing Pet Show.

They met.

The boy caught the fly in a jar.

"A pet!" he said.

The fly was mad.

He wanted to be free.

He stomped his foot

and said— BUZZ!

The boy was surprised.

He said, "You know my name!

You are the smartest pet in

the world!"

Chapter 2

Buzz took the fly home.

"This is my pet," Buzz said to Mom and Dad.

"He is smart. He can say
my name. Listen!"

Buzz opened the jar.

The fly flew out.

"Flies can't be pets!" said
Dad. "They are pests!"
He got the fly swatter.
The fly cried—

BUZZ!

And Buzz came to the rescue.

"You are right," said Dad.

"This fly <u>is</u> smart!"

"He needs a name," said Mom.

Buzz thought for a minute.

"Fly Guy," said Buzz.

And Fly Guy said— BUZZ!

It was time for lunch.
Buzz gave Fly Guy
something to eat.
Fly Guy was happy.

Chapter 3

Buzz took Fly Guy to

The Amazing Pet Show.

The judges laughed.

"Flies can't be pets," they said.

"Flies are pests!"

Buzz was sad.

He opened the jar.

"Shoo, Fly Guy," he said.

"Flies can't be pets."

But Fly Guy liked Buzz.

He had an idea.

He did some fancy flying.

The judges were amazed.
"The fly can do tricks," they
said. "But flies can't be pets."

Then Fly Guy said—

The judges were more amazed. "The fly knows the boy's name," they said. "But flies can't be pets."

Fly Guy flew high, high, high into the sky!

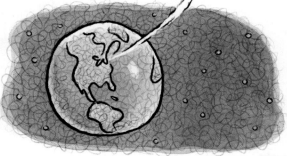

Then he dived down, down, down into the jar.

"The fly knows his jar!" the
judges said. "This fly is a pet!"
They let Fly Guy in the show.

He even won an award.

And so began a
beautiful friendship.

Dig Deeper

Use Clues to Analyze the Text

Use these pages to learn about Understanding Characters and Author's Word Choice. Then read **Hi! Fly Guy** again.

Understanding Characters

Buzz and Fly Guy are **characters** in **Hi! Fly Guy.** What does Buzz do to help Fly Guy? What does Fly Guy do to help Buzz? Use what the characters do and say as text evidence to figure out their feelings. Pictures can give clues, too. List details in a chart to help you describe the characters.

Words	Actions	Feelings

Author's Word Choice

Writers choose words that help you know how things look, feel, sound, smell, or taste. The author says that the fly went looking for something **slimy**. What do you picture in your mind when you read the word **slimy**?

What word tells what Fly Guy sounds like? What other words in the story describe what things are like?

Your Turn

RETURN TO THE ESSENTIAL QUESTION

 Turn and Talk

How can insects be helpful? Talk about real insects and then about Fly Guy. Use story words and pictures to help you tell how Buzz took care of Fly Guy. Then use text evidence to describe how Fly Guy helped Buzz.

Classroom Conversation

Talk about these questions with your class.

1 How is Fly Guy like pets you know about?

2 How can you tell Fly Guy likes Buzz?

3 What do you think Fly Guy and Buzz will do next?

WRITE ABOUT READING ....  my WriteSmart

Response Write sentences that tell why you think Fly Guy is a good pet. Give reasons why you feel as you do. Use text evidence from the story for ideas.

Writing Tip

Use words such as **because** and **so** to give reasons for your opinions.

POETRY

✅ GENRE

Poetry uses the sounds of words to help describe feelings. Which rhyming words make the poems fun to hear and say?

✅ TEXT FOCUS

Rhythm is a pattern of beats, like music. Clap along with the rhythm of the poems.

Busy Bugs

How do you think this poet got the idea to write a snail poem? Read how the snail says hello to the Sun.

Caracol, caracol

Caracol, caracol,
saca tus cuernos al sol.

To a Snail

Poke your head out, little one.
Time to say, "Good morning, Sun!"

traditional Spanish rhyme

You can look for bugs under rocks, on leaves, or in the grass. Look for bugs with wings flying in the air.

Song of the Bugs

Some bugs pinch
And some bugs creep
Some bugs buzz themselves to sleep
Buzz Buzz Buzz Buzz
This is the song of the bugs.

Some bugs fly
When the moon is high
Some bugs make a light in the sky
Flicker, flicker firefly
This is the song of the bugs.

by Margaret Wise Brown

On almost any rainy day you will be sure to see worms. Watch them move!

Worm

Squiggly
Wiggly
Wriggly
Jiggly
Ziggly
Higgly
Piggly
Worm.

Watch it wiggle
Watch it wriggle
See it squiggle
See it squirm!

by Mary Ann Hoberman

Respond to Poetry

Write a poem about a bug you know. Use rhyming words. Use words to tell what the bug looks like and how it moves. Memorize a rhyme or poem. Say it to the class.

Compare Texts

Read Together

TEXT TO TEXT

Write a Poem Write a poem about Fly Guy like one of the poems in **Busy Bugs.** Use words that tell how things look, sound, smell, taste, or feel.

TEXT TO SELF

Write a Caption Draw a picture of your favorite bug. Write a caption that tells how it moves.

TEXT TO WORLD

Discuss Bugs Tell what kinds of bugs are in your state. Use sources to help you find out more about them. Work with classmates to write facts.

Grammar

Adverbs Adverbs are words that describe verbs. They can tell **how, where, when,** or **how much** something is. Many, but not all, adverbs end with **ly**.

Read Together

Adverbs	
How	The boat moves quickly in the water. They carefully steered the boat.
Where	They're here! The water splashed everywhere.
When	The bugs woke up early in the morning. They went to bed late.
How much	They kicked a ball very hard. The ball flew by too fast.

Work with a partner. Read each sentence and find the adverb. Decide if it tells how, where, when, or how much. Then say a new sentence, using the adverb.

1. Ned slowly unpacked the picnic basket.

2. His friends walk to get there.

3. Fred was very tired from the trip.

4. Bea cheerfully told a joke.

5. They want to have picnics often.

Connect Grammar to Writing

When you revise your writing, look for places where you can add adverbs.

Opinion Writing

✔ **Evidence** Before writing an **opinion paragraph,** list your opinion and reasons for it. Think of examples to explain your reasons.

Tara wanted to tell why Fly Guy is a good pet. To help find good examples, she looked through **Hi! Fly Guy** again.

Explore a Topic

Prewriting Checklist

✔ Did I list my opinion?

✔ Did I give a few good reasons?

✔ Do my examples explain my reasons?

✔ Did I write my idea for a closing sentence?

Read Tara's plan. What is her opinion? What are her reasons? Plan and draft your paragraph. Use the Checklist.

Planning Chart

My Opinion
Fly Guy = good pet

First Reason
Fly Guy is smart

Examples
knows Buzz's name
flies back into his jar

Second Reason
helps Buzz

Example
does tricks to get in the pet show

Closing
Fly Guy is a good pet <u>and</u> friend

Talk About Words
Nouns are words that name people, animals, things, or places. Work with a partner. Find the blue words that are nouns. Use them in complete sentences.

Words to Know

Read Together

▶ Read each **Context Card.**

▶ Use a blue word to tell about something you did.

1 **loved**

They **loved** being part of the soccer team.

2 **everyone**

Everyone had fun at the game.

3 brothers

The brothers are on the same team.

4 field

The field was wet after the rain.

5 sorry

The girl was sorry she couldn't play today.

6 only

The Reds are ahead by only one point.

7 people

People were happy after the game.

8 most

The team cheered most for their coach.

Read and Comprehend

Read Together

☑ **TARGET SKILL**

Main Idea and Details A selection is about one big idea, the **topic**. The **main idea** is the most important idea about the topic. **Details** are facts and other bits of information an author uses to tell more about the main idea. Details help make events and ideas clearer. List the main idea and details about a topic on a web.

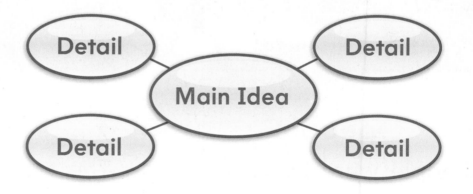

☑ **TARGET STRATEGY**

Summarize As you read, stop to retell the important events in your own words.

Teamwork

The players on a soccer team work together to move the ball down the field to get a goal. It is up to each person to try his or her best. You will read about a girl who plays on a team in **Winners Never Quit!**

💬 Talk About It

What do you know about being part of a team? What would you like to know? Share your ideas. What did you learn?

ANCHOR TEXT

MIA HAMM
Winners Never Quit!

Illustrations by
Carol Thompson

✓ GENRE

Narrative nonfiction tells a true story. As you read, look for:
- ▸ a setting that is real
- ▸ real people as characters

Meet the Author

Mia Hamm

Mia Hamm went from playing football to soccer at age fourteen. She became one of the best women's soccer players ever. She knows what it takes to be a good teammate!

Meet the Illustrator

Carol Thompson

Carol Thompson has won many awards for illustrating children's picture books. She also makes greeting cards. She lives in England with her family.

Winners Never Quit!

by Mia Hamm
illustrated by Carol Thompson

ESSENTIAL QUESTION

Why is teamwork important in school or sports?

Mia loved basketball.

Mia loved baseball.

But most of all, Mia loved
soccer. She played every
day with her brothers
and sisters.

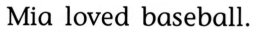

Tap, tap, tap. Her toes kept the ball right
where she wanted it. Then, *smack*! She'd
kick the ball straight into the net. **Goal!**
Everyone on her team would cheer.

But sometimes it didn't work that way.
One day, no matter how hard she tried,
Mia couldn't score a goal.

The ball sailed to
the left of the net.

Or to the right.

Or her sister Lovdy,
the goalie, saved the
ball with her hands.

No goal.

No cheering.

"Too bad, Mia," her brother Garrett said. "Better luck next time!"

But Mia didn't want better luck next time. She wanted better luck *now*.

"I Quit!"

Mia said.

"You can't quit!" Lovdy
said. "Then we'll only have
two people on our team."

"Come on, Mia," her sister
Caroline pleaded. "You always
quit when you start losing."

"Just keep playing, Mia,"
Garrett said. "It'll be fun."

But losing wasn't fun. Mia stomped
back to the house.

"Quitter!"

"Quitter!" Lovdy yelled.
Mia didn't care.
She'd rather quit than lose.

The next day, Mia ran outside, ready to play soccer. When she got there, the game had already started.

"Hey!" she yelled. "Why didn't you wait for me?"

Garrett stopped playing.

"Sorry, Mia," he said. "But quitters can't play on my team."

"Yeah," said Lovdy. "If you can't learn to lose, you can't play."

Garrett passed the ball to
Tiffany. Martin ran to steal it.
Tiffany dashed around him
and took a shot at the goal.
Lovdy blocked it.

Mia just stood
by the side and
watched.

The next day, Garrett picked Mia first
for his team.

Mia got the ball. She dribbled down
the field. *Smack!* She kicked the ball
toward the goal.

And Lovdy caught it.

No goal.

No cheering.

"Too bad, Mia," Garrett said. "Better luck next time."

Mia felt tears in her eyes.

"She's going to quit," whispered Lovdy. "I knew it."

Mia still hated losing. But she didn't hate losing as much as she loved soccer.

"Ready to play?" asked Garrett.

Mia nodded.

Garrett grinned at her. He passed her the ball.

Mia ran down the field. Tap, tap, tap with her toes. The ball stayed right with her, like a friend. She got ready to kick it into the goal.

Mia kicked the ball as hard as she could.

Maybe she'd score the goal. Maybe she wouldn't.

But she was playing.

And that was more important than winning or losing . . .

because winners never quit!

ANALYZE THE TEXT

Main Idea and Details What is the main idea of the selection? What do the characters do to show the main idea?

Dig Deeper

Use Clues to Analyze the Text

Use these pages to learn about Main Idea and Details and Narrative Nonfiction. Then read **Winners Never Quit!** again.

Main Idea and Details

Think about the **topic**, or the one big idea, that **Winners Never Quit!** is about. What is the **main idea** the author tells about the topic? The author gives bits of information to tell more about the main idea. What details help you know more about being a good team player? Show the main idea and details in a web.

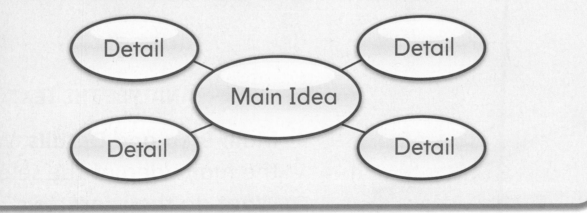

Genre: Narrative Nonfiction

Winners Never Quit! tells about events in the life of a real person named Mia Hamm. Here she is! Her story has a real setting and gives information. It tells about events in the order that they really happened.

The facts and events are told like a story. How did the author make **Winners Never Quit!** a fun way to learn true information about her life?

Your Turn

RETURN TO THE ESSENTIAL QUESTION

 **Turn and Talk**

Why is teamwork important in school or sports? Talk about what makes a good team player. Use text evidence and details that the author uses to back up her main idea. Take turns speaking.

Classroom Conversation

Talk about these questions with your class.

1. Why does Mia quit at first? Have you ever felt like she did? What did you do?

2. How does Garrett help Mia?

3. How does Mia learn that it is better to play than to quit?

WRITE ABOUT READING ··········

Response Write sentences to tell Mia why she should not give up. What advice can you give her? What text evidence can you use? First, talk to a partner about your ideas. Then use some of your partner's ideas and your own ideas to make your writing clear.

Writing Tip

Stay on topic. Add details to help explain your ideas.

INFORMATIONAL TEXT

Read Together

Be a Team Player

☑ **GENRE**

Informational text gives facts about a topic. Find facts about being on a team in this social studies text.

☑ **TEXT FOCUS**

A **checklist** is a list of names or things to think about or do. What do you learn from the checklist on p. 184?

Be a Team Player

Have you ever loved playing on a team? Most people have lots of fun on a team.

All kinds of people play on teams. Sisters and brothers play. Friends and cousins play.

There are all kinds of teams. Some people play baseball or basketball. Some play soccer or volleyball. People may play on a field or on a court.

No matter what kind of team it is, it's important to be a good team player. Try not to feel sorry if you lose a game. Everyone loses sometimes. It's only important to try your best and have fun.

Here is a checklist of things to remember when you play on a team.

Be a Team Player.

✔ Pay attention to the coach.
✔ Follow the rules.
✔ Do your best.
✔ Don't quit.
✔ Have fun!

Compare Texts

Read Together

TEXT TO TEXT

Talk About It What do you need to do when you play on a team? Did Mia become a good team player? Tell why you think so.

TEXT TO SELF

Write a Poem Write a poem about being part of a team. Use words that tell about sights, sounds, and feelings.

TEXT TO WORLD

Connect to Social Studies Name a time when you need to be a team player. Draw a picture to show your idea. Describe it clearly to a partner.

Grammar

Adjectives That Compare Add **er** to adjectives to compare two. Add **est** to compare more than two.

Read Together

Compare Two
Meg is **tall<u>er</u>** than Jon.

Compare More Than Two
Abe is the **tall<u>est</u>** goalie of all.

tall   **taller**   **tallest**

Write adjectives from the boxes to finish the sentences. Use another sheet of paper.

| small | smaller | smallest |

1. We have a very __?__ soccer team.

2. Our team is the __?__ team in town.

3. Brad's team is __?__ than Eva's team.

| fast | faster | fastest |

4. I am __?__ than Kyla.

5. Rob is the __?__ runner in the game.

Connect Grammar to Writing

When you revise your writing, try adding some adjectives that compare.

Opinion Writing

my WriteSmart

☑ **Organization** A good **opinion paragraph** has a topic sentence that tells an opinion. A closing sentence retells the opinion in new words. Tara drafted her opinion paragraph. She indented the first word. Then she added a closing sentence.

Read Together

Revised Draft

That makes Buzz happy. ∧ Fly Guy is a good pet for Buzz and a good friend!

Revising Checklist

☑ Does my topic sentence tell my opinion?

☑ Did I give good reasons for my opinion?

☑ Do I need more examples for my reasons?

☑ Does my closing sentence retell my opinion?

Final Copy

A Good Pet

Hi! <u>Fly Guy</u> is about a good pet named Fly Guy. He is a good pet because he is smart. Fly Guy knows Buzz's name. He also knows where his home is and flies back into his jar. Another reason is that Fly Guy helps Buzz. Fly Guy does fancy flying and other tricks to get into the pet show. He shows the judges that he really is a pet and should be in the show. Fly Guy wins an award. That makes Buzz happy. Fly Guy is a good pet for Buzz <u>and</u> a good friend!

Write an Opinion Paragraph

Read
Together

TASK Look at **What Can You Do?** and **Winners Never Quit!** Then write an opinion paragraph. Tell younger students which activity you think is the best one to learn how to do.

PLAN

myNotebook

Gather Information Talk with a group about the two texts. Which activities do you like? Tell why. Then write ideas for your opinion paragraph in a chart.

Use the tools in your eBook to remember important details from the texts.

- Pick the activity from the texts that you think is the best one to learn. Write your opinion.

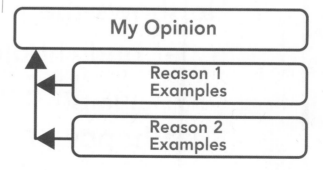

My Opinion

Reason 1
Examples

Reason 2
Examples

- What are good reasons for your opinion? Find examples in the texts to explain your reasons.

Write Your Opinion Paragraph Use your chart for ideas. Follow these steps.

Write your draft in *my*WriteSmart.

My Opinion

First, write a topic sentence that tells your opinion about the best activity to learn.

⬇

Reason 1

Write a good reason for your opinion.

I think _____ because _____.

Write examples from the texts to help make your reason clear. Use different kinds of sentences to make your writing interesting. Use exclamations to show strong feelings.

Learn to _____. It will help you _____.

When you learn _____, you'll feel _____!

⬇

Reason 2

Write another good reason for your opinion. Write examples to explain.

⬇

Closing

Write a closing sentence for your paragraph. Tell your opinion again using different words. You can also use your own idea.

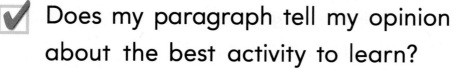
Review Your Draft Read your writing and make it better. Use the Checklist.

Ask a partner to read your draft. Talk about how you can make it better.

☑ Does my paragraph tell my opinion about the best activity to learn?

☑ Did I give good reasons?

☑ Did I use examples to help explain my reasons?

☑ Does my closing sentence give the paragraph an ending?

☑ Did I use different kinds of sentences with the correct end marks?

PRESENT

Share Write or type a final copy of your opinion paragraph. Add a picture. Pick a way to share.

- Read your paragraph. Record it.

- Read it to a younger student.

Words to Know

Unit 6   High-Frequency Words

26 The Dot

teacher	bear
studied	above
surprised	even
toward	pushed

27 What Can You Do?

different	high
near	always
enough	once
stories	happy

28 "The Kite"

second	heard
ball	large
across	cried
head	should

29 Hi! Fly Guy

caught	minute
took	idea
listen	beautiful
thought	friendship

30 Winners Never Quit!

loved	sorry
everyone	only
brothers	people
field	most

Glossary

A

already

Already means before this. My brother was **already** at school by the time my bus arrived.

award

An **award** is a kind of prize for being good at something. My friend won an **award** for winning the spelling bee.

B

binoculars

Binoculars are something you look through to make things look closer. Seth looked through the **binoculars** and saw an eagle in a tree.

blank

Blank means with no writing on it. The sheet of paper was **blank**.

C

captain

A **captain** is a kind of leader. Suzie is the **captain** of our swim team.

chapter

A long piece of writing may be divided into parts called **chapters**. I just read the last **chapter** in my book.

computers

A **computer** is a machine that works with words, pictures, and numbers. We have two **computers** in our classroom.

D

dribbled

To **dribble** means to use your hands or feet to move a ball from one place to another. Brian **dribbled** the ball past the other players.

F

fancy

The word **fancy** can describe movements that are complex or surprising. The dancers used some **fancy** footwork.

float

To **float** means to move on top of water. I like to **float** on a raft in the pool.

G

gazing

To **gaze** means to look at something. When Ms. Tam found Ben, he was **gazing** out the window.

goalie

A **goalie** is the player who tries to keep the other team from scoring points. Lupe is the best **goalie** on our soccer team.

guy

The word **guy** is informal and is similar to the meaning of *fellow*. That puppy is a cute little **guy**.

J

junk
Junk is something that people do not want. Max and his mom took the **junk** out with the rest of the trash.

L

laughter
Laughter is what you hear when people think something is funny. The story was so funny that we all burst into **laughter**.

N

noticed
To **notice** is to see or hear something. Jason **noticed** the spot on his shirt.

P

perhaps
Perhaps means maybe. **Perhaps** our class will go there on a field trip.

R

rather
Rather is used when you like one thing more than another. I would **rather** ride a bike than walk.

rescue
If you come to someone's **rescue**, you save them from danger or a problem. My pal forgot his math book, but I came to his **rescue** and lent him mine.

S

something

Something means any thing. I wanted to wear **something** red that day.

squiggle

A **squiggle** is a wavy line. My little brother made a **squiggle** with the red crayon.

straight

If something is **straight**, it has no turns or curves. I used a ruler to make my lines **straight**.

swirly

Swirly means in a curving way. Lily used a brush to make **swirly** blue lines on her painting.

Acknowledgments

"Caracol, caracol/To a Snail" from *¡Pío Peep!: Traditional Spanish Nursery Rhymes*, selected by Alma Flor Ada & F. Isabel Campoy. Spanish compilation copyright ©2003 by Alma Flor Ada & Isabel Campoy. English adaptation copyright ©2003 by Alice Schertle. Reprinted by permission of HarperCollins Publishers.

Days with Frog and Toad by Arnold Lobel. Copyright ©1979 by Arnold Lobel. All rights reserved. Reprinted by permission of HarperCollins Children's Books, a division of HarperCollins Publishers.

The Dot by Peter H. Reynolds. Copyright ©2003 by Peter H. Reynolds. Reprinted by permission of the publisher Candlewick Press Inc. and Pippin Properties, Inc.

Hi! Fly Guy by Tedd Arnold. Copyright ©2005 by Tedd Arnold, Reprinted by Scholastic Inc. SCHOLASTIC'S Material shall not be published, retransmitted, broadcast, downloaded, modified or adapted (rewritten), manipulated, reproduced or otherwise distributed and/or exploited in any way without the prior written authorization of Scholastic Inc.

"Song of the Bugs" from *Nibble, Nibble* by Margaret Wise Brown. Copyright ©1959 by William R. Scott, Inc., renewed 1987 by Roberta Brown Rauch. Reprinted by permission of HarperCollins Publishers.

What Can You Do? by Shelley Rotner and Sheila Kelley, with photographs by Shelley Rotner. Coauthor of text and photographs copyright ©2001 by Shelley Rotner. Coauthor of text copyright ©2001 by Sheila Kelley. Reprinted by the permission of Millbrook Press, a division of Lerner Publishing Group. Inc. All rights reserved.

Winners Never Quit! by Mia Hamm, illustrated by Carol Thompson. Text and illustrations copyright ©2004 by Mia Hamm and Byron Preiss Visual Publications, Inc. All rights reserved. Reprinted by permission of HarperCollins Children's Books, a division of HarperCollins Publishers.

"Worm" from *A Little Book of Little Beasts* by Mary Ann Hoberman. Copyright ©1973, renewed 2001 by Mary Ann Hoberman. Reprinted by permission of Gina Maccoby Literary Agency.

Credits

Placement Key:

(r) right, (l) left, (c) center, (t) top, (b) bottom, (bg) background

Photo Credits

3 (cl) ©Francis G. Mayer/Corbis; 4 (cl) ©Shelley Rotner, Photographer; 7 (cl) ©Paul Barton/Corbis; 8 ©PatrikOntkovic/Shutterstock; 9 ©Rawpixel/Shutterstock; ©Blend Images/TIPS USA LLC; 10 (br) ©Simon Marcus/Corbis; 10 ©Andreanna Seymore/Getty Images; 10 ©Francis G. Mayer/Corbis; 11 (cr) ©Mia Foster/PhotoEdit; 11 ©D. Hurst/Alamy Images; 11 ©Darrin Klimek/Digital Vision/Getty Images; 11 ©Howard Grey/Digital Vision/Getty Images; 11 ©Bettmann/Corbis; 12 Dmytro Tolokonov/Alamy; 35 MBI/Alamy; 37 Cultura Creative/Alamy; 38 (b) ©Chain Ring Creative Services, Inc.; 38 ©Francis G. Mayer/Corbis; 39 ©Francis G. Mayer/Corbis; 40 (c) ©Preserve Bottle Village Committee; 40 (bg) ©Preserve Bottle Village Committee; 41 ©Westend61/Getty Images; 41 ©Francis G. Mayer/Corbis; 42 ©Ariel Skelley/Corbis; 46 ©JGI/Jamie Grill/Getty Images; 46 ©Ariel Skelley/Riser/Getty Images; 46 ©Shelley Rotner, Photographer; 47 ©Cassy Cohen/PhotoEdit; 47 (cr) ©Julie Habel/Corbis; 47 ©Tony Anderson/Taxi/Getty Images; 47 ©Cindy Charles/PhotoEdit; 47 ©Ariel Skelley/Blend Images/Getty Images; 47 ©Corbis; 49 LAWRENCE MIGDALE/Getty Images; 50 (tr) ©Shelley Rotner, Photographer; 50 (tl) ©Shelley Rotner, Photographer; 70 (tl) ©Shelley Rotner, Photographer; 71 Steve Hamblin/Alamy; 73 (tr) ©Shelley Rotner, Photographer; 77 (b) © VStock/Alamy; 77 ©Getty Images; 77 Getty Images Royalty Free; 77 ©Stockbyte/Getty Images; 77 ©Shelley Rotner, Photographer; 78 ©Ken Chernus/Taxi/Getty Center; 79 ©Janine Wiedel Photolibrary/Alamy Images; 82 ©imac/Alamy Images; 82 ©Tom Stewart/Corbis; 83 ©Mary Kate Denny/Getty Images; 83 ©Mary Kate Denny/Getty Images; 83 (tl) ©Blend Images/Alamy Images; 83 (bl) ©Ariel Skelley/Blend Images/Getty Images; 83 (cr) ©Ken Redding/Corbis; 83 (cl) ©Radius Images/Alamy Images; 84 © Ariel Skelley/Getty Images; 103 © BYphoto/Alamy; 106 ©Ruediger Knobloch/Corbis; 107 (br) ©Ariel Skelley/Getty Images;